FREE BORN

Ngozi Olivia Osuoha

also by Ngozi Olivia Osuoha

The Transformation Train
Letter to My Unborn
Sensation
Tropical Escape (with Amos O. Ojwang')
Fruits from the Poetry Planet
Poetic Grenade
Whispers of the Biafran Skeleton
Chains
Raindrops
Eclipse of Tides

Freeborn

poems by
Ngozi Olivia Osuoha

Poetic Justice Books & Arts
Port Saint Lucie, Florida

©2019 Ngozi Olivia Osuoha

book design and layout: SpiNDec, Port Saint Lucie, FL
cover design: Kris Haggblom

All rights reserved.

No part of this book may be used or reproduced in any manner whatsoever without written permission except in the case of brief quotations embodied in critical articles and reviews. Members of educational institutions and organizations wishing to photocopy any of the work for classroom use, or authors, artists and publishers who would like to obtain permission for any material in the work, should contact the publisher.

Published by Poetic Justice Books
Port Saint Lucie, Florida
www.poeticjusticebooks.com

ISBN: 978-1-950433-16-2

10 9 8 7 6 5 4 3 2

dedicated to
AFRICA

Freeborn

Love 1
Dream 2
Ambition 3
Peace 4
Atrocity 5
Superstition 6
Conquest 7
Anger 8
Malice 9
Honesty 10
Here for You 11
My Angel 12
Courage 13
Peak 14
Wonders 15
Autism 16
Law 17
Rumour 18
Gossip 19
Poverty 20
Tradition 21
Wilderness 22
Pride 23
Shadow 24
My Blue Robe 25
The Farmer 26
The Green Tree 27
How Dare You 28
Let It Rain 29
I Am Not a Butterfly 30
My Little Friend 31

Ghost	32
Cold	33
God's Love	34
Culture	35
Religion	36
Chains	37
Freeborn	38
Angel	39
Happy Birthday	40
Rebirth	41
Congratulations	42
Parenting	43
Emacipation	44
Time	45
Choice	46
Money	47
Take Me to the Mountains	48
Marriage	49
Honey	50
acknowledgement	53
about the author	55

Freeborn

Love

When I see my heartthrob
I will know,
When I see my enemy
I will flee,
But when I see a deceiver
I may learn.

O my dear love
Feel free to mingle
O my sweetheart
Feel free to fly,
For love is real
So real to be true.

When I am lonely
I will sing a song
When I am needy
I will say a prayer,
When I am bored
I will keep busy
That way, I will not miss you
Because I know you are real.

Dream

You are my dream
Down this tracky stream
You are my team
High above this realm.

Dreams of yesteryears
Hopes of ages past
Dreams of countless morrows
Songs of tearless furrows.

O my dear dream
Beyond my bed,
O my dear dream
Beyond my sleep.

I fall down to live
I bow down to worship
That way I am happy
For tomorrow.

Yet, my dream
Yes, my dream
That's me, my dream.

Ambition

My life is a song
Unheard, unwritten, unknown
My life is a journey
Far, mysterious, magical
My life is a tower
High, on top the sky
That way, I focus on my ambition.

I have my rendition
With an edition
I have an admonition
With my own registration.

White, black, green or yellow
Purple, blue, brown or indigo
My ambition is a key
With a tone for tunes
Melodious like a flute
Keen, beautiful and absolute.

Through the wilderness
Amidst the desert
You find me with my ambition.

Peace

Peace is a war
Locked in the cave,
Peace is a trouble
Sealed in the cage,
Peace is a pain
Silenced in vain.

Peace is a veil
A covering of deceit
Peace is a frame
A holder of image,
Peace is a skeleton
A shade of flesh
Peace is a space
It has no place.

When the sea is troubled
And the mountain, angered
When the land is struck
And wind, disturbed
Peace runs, hides and travels
Then you know his strength
A little but most insecure.

Atrocity

Lo, he comes in the wind
Speeding in full strength
Lo, he sweeps the land
Raging in candid spoil
There, he goes in might
As though his, is the world.

 Look up and see him
Look down and feel him
Look beyond, he is there
Look yonder, search farther
He is the air we breathe
He is the water we thirst for
Lo, he is atrocity.

No one cares about him
Because everyone is in tune,
No one speaks against him
Because everyone is carried away
Lo, he serves our breakfast
Lo, he serves our lunch
Lo, he prepares our dinner
Lo, no one dares hurt him.

Superstition

The fear of the unknown
With traces of truth
The belief of the unseen
With traits of lies
The doubt of the happening
With chances of coincidence.

Superstition, the killer of dreams
The hedge against freedom
The edge between life and death.

Yesterday is gone
Today is here,
Tomorrow is coming
Yesterday is dead
Today is living
Tomorrow is alive.

But all can live
When any can leave
But all can leave
When any can live
Superstition, the rope to dent a robe.

Conquest

Our victory is a joy
That nothing can cloy
But our joy is victory
That something may cloy
Victory, joy and conquest
Three brothers in one
It depends who fights others.

The conquest is a threat
The threat is a conquest
The conquest can be threatened
And the threat can be conquered.

Our conquest is our victory
Our victory is a conquest
Our joy, our conquest
Our conquest, our joy.

When we maintain our conquest
It threatens our enemy
When we threaten our enemy
We glow in joy
Though nothing is ever guaranteed.

Anger

When the best man is angry
Fear him,
When the worst man is angry
Run away.

When your angel is sad
Feed him,
When your demon is bitter
Watch out

When our friend is jealous
Be careful,
When your foe is envious
Take cover

When our home is happy
Merry,
When your people are outrageous
Mourn.

Fear him, run away, feed him
Watch out, be careful, take cover
Merry, mourn, for such is life.

Malice

When you are hated
You are underrated
When you are invalid
Your points are not solid,
When you are nobody
They paint you muddy.

The heart is beyond the face
And the face is above the heart,
Our utterances differ
And our actions linger,
Those who do not love us
Tend to destabilize our focus.

Grudges born malice
Malice incubate grudges
Both commit murder
Within and across the border,
So none is so holy
When all is unruly
But anyone heady
Has many things shady.

Honesty

A joke of the century
Buried in the cemetery,
A play in the theater
Entertaining the cinema
Honesty, a forgone alternative.

Sold, hidden, lost
Bought, suppressed, murdered
Killed, forgotten, forbidden
Banished, vanquished, finished
Honesty, a lost identity.

The root of hate
The show of wickedness
The cause of enmity
Honesty, a load of terror
Threatening the peacekeeper.

Swallow it and be free
Tell it and die
Mock and live
Keep it and disappear
Honesty, a journey of no return

Here for You

My fragile heart is for you
And my pure love for you,
My peaceful heart searches
And my lovely soul yearns.

Lo, I am here
Whispering to your ears
Lo, I wait
Wondering if you care.

My poor frame is strong
And my beautiful mind prays
Lo, I am here
Wandering not to stray.

Dear love, my heart is real
Sweet heart, I am here for you
Please let me in.

My Angel

You are so kind
And down to earth
You are so tolerant
And fair to me,
O my angel
I want to be like you
Please help me dear,
Let me grow more
And be an angel
Just like you.

Courage

This ridge
Is a fridge
Freezing our bridge
So if the cartridge
Kills the ostrich
And the porridge
Poisons the partridge
Then our carriage
May find no courage.

Peak

Seek my cheek
And pick my week
Check my lick
Not to be sick.

As a freak
Reaching the peak
Let nothing leak.

O dear seeker
Do not be weak,
O dear maker
Take us to the peak.

Wonders

Soot for sooth
Smoke for coke
Stone for tone
Grave for wave
Toil for oil
Hate for date,
Wonders on wonders.

Clay for way
Delay for pay
Lay for say
Blame for game
Lame for fame
Mood for good
Wonders upon wonders.

Trouble for double
Cuddle for kindle
Hurdle in bundle
Puddle for candle,
Wonders O wonders.

Autism

I sing and dance and play
I smile and laugh and frown
That's when I am lucky enough.

Born in a bend to bend the bend in a bend
Deep the steep, a cliff and rift
I see a confluence.

When unlucky, they push me out
When unfortunate, they sidetrack me
When ungodly, they shame me
When unwanted, they leave me behind
When tired, they get rid of me.

But I am unique and talented
Hidden, untapped, unharnessed
Yes, I am a deity
But they tag me autism.

Law

Law obeys money
And disrespects lack
Law serves riches
And abuses poverty
Law answers wealth
And belittles want,
Law honours health
And dishonours sickness
Law, the adverse of life.

Law monitors fame
And disgraces lame,
Law safeguards game
And exposes tame,
Law builds courage
And dismantles fear
Law hails boldness
And angers timidity
Law, the coat of a nobody.

Law, for the downtrodden
Law, for the segregated
Law, for the discriminated
Law, just for the common man.

Rumour

There is an odour
That goes viral
It targets its victim
To dent and diminish.

There is a rumour
It bears no splendour
It hurts its victim
To discredit and abuse.

There is a fowl play
That spreads its wings
It sells its victims
To tarnish and vanquish.

There is a rumour
Sometimes intentional
Sometimes international
Sometimes interdenominational
Sometimes interpersonal
It subdues, it angers
It detriments, it paints
It sours, it saddens
There is this rumour
It hurts its victims,
In short, in fact, it kills.

Gossip

Idle thinkers, wasting their time
Piling up stories like mountains
Fomenting lies like truths,
Bearing witnesses like necessary
They swear, they vow, they affirm.

Gossipers gossip people
Telling the tales of unimportance
Tending to gain attention
Fighting to earn fame
Struggling for respect.

Stories untrue and unreal
Hearsay, unheard and unconfirmed
Intentions, bitter to batter
Reasons, wondering and wondering.

Gossip, the trail of hate
The track of inferiority complex
The bid to belong, unfortunate
Gossip, a table of irrelevance
A gathering of vultures
Feasting on something dirty like them.

Poverty

This is a mirror
That reflects horror
This is a river
That sinks liver.

This is a table
That holds the cable,
This is the garden
That is hidden.

Beyond it, is a hand
Buried deep in the land
Behind it, is a band
Burdened without a stand.

Poverty is a bug
Even under the rug
It is a lice
That eats up the rice,
It can never be nice.

Poverty is a curse
Drying the purse,
Poverty is an impulse
That can make one pause.

Tradition

The one we worship
And dance with a hip
The one we ship
And seal our lip
Tradition, a cup of tea.

Tradition, the bundle of fate
A footage of bondage
In the lineage of mirage
A clue of agedness
That surrounds sadness.

Tradition, a study of ancient
A dealing pure and impure
Coated, diluted, neutralized.

It could be new
It could be old
It could be dew
It could be bold
It could be few
It could be cold.

Wilderness

Life is a wilderness
With some happiness
Life is a wilderness
With some sadness.

Life is a wilderness
With some loneliness,
Life is a wilderness
With some fairness.

Life is a wilderness
With some ugliness,
Life is a wilderness
With some mildness.

Life is a wilderness
With some meekness
Life is a wilderness
With some weakness.

Life is a wilderness
With some roughness,
Life is a wilderness
With some toughness.

Pride

It is wide
Like the tide
It is a ride
With nothing to hide.

Pride in the noon
A broad day light
Proud in the dark
Darkness beyond night.

A choke in the air
To tighten the neck
A poke in the hair
To quicken the peck.

A lonely poor heart
Twinkling like the star
Far beyond the sky
Heavy like the cloud.

A goddess in the sea
Mighty like a whirlwind
A queen in the land
Beauty like no other.

Shadow

Walking fast, walking slow
Singing deep, singing low
You are there.

Long, short, moderate
Dark, light
Gone, there
Disappeared or reappeared.

My partner, my friend
My mimicker, my learner
My leader, my follower
You are there, you are here.

My shadow is right
My shadow is left
My shadow is right
My shadow is wrong
Where I am, who I am
What I am, when I am
How I am, is my shadow.

My Blue Robe

My dear blue robe
Long, sweeping
Touching down, sparking
Blue, blue, blue.

My blue robe
Beautiful and neat
Dazzling diamond
Shinning star.

My blue robe
Colourful, artful needful
Pure, spick and span.

O my dear blue robe
On my stool, I sit
Watching and waving
Smiling and praying.

My blue robe
Flying across the globe
O you are royal
Hence, I am loyal.

The Farmer

O dear farmer
You are strong
And strong,
You till the land
And plant the seed
You water the land
And weed the seed,
You prune the farm
And get some harm
But you give us food
When you harvest.

Your harvest is great
It pays your sweat,
Your harvest is green
It booms like teen.

O dear farmer
Please, please the earth
O dear farmer
Please plant more for us
Let us live and jolly.

The Green Tree

You are bound to be fruitful
Do not be barren.

You are bound to be joyful
Do not be saddened.

You are bound to be beautiful
Do not be ugly.

You are bound to be lovely
Do not be unruly.

You are bound to be holy
Do not be ungodly.

You are bound to be calm
Heal with your balm.

You are bound to be lively
Do not be madly.

The green tree
You are bound to be free.

How Dare You

How dare you pretend
To be a friend?

How dare you produce
Just to reduce?

How dare you associate
To dissociate?

How dare you announce
To denounce?

How dare you mourn
Never to return?

How dare you collide
Just to divide?

How dare you bind
In order to be blind?

How dare you succumb
Just to be dumb,
How dare you?

Let It Rain

If my pen is thick
Then let it stick,
If my ink is cool
Then let it fool.

If my words are real
Then let them heal
If my message is true
Then let them screw.

If my bed is divine
Let it be my wine,
If my coat is clean
Let it wean.

If my wish is big
Let it dig,
If my prayer is sound
Then let it pound
If my cloud is loud
Then let it rain.

I Am not a Butterfly

I am not a butterfly
But I can fly
I am not a butterfly
But I can colour.

I am not a butterfly
But I can try,
I am not a butterfly
But I can cry.

I am not a butterfly
But I have a pillar
I am not a butterfly
But I am a tiller.

I am not a butterfly
But I have wings
I am not a butterfly
But I have kings
I am not a butterfly
But I eat bread
I am not a butterfly
But I crown my head.

My Little Friend

I have a little friend
She looks like a princess
And dreams like a queen.

I have a little friend
She eats like an angel
And drinks like a goddess.

I have a little friend
She prays like a warrior
And never feels inferior.

I have a little friend
She sings like choir
And brings down glory.

I have a little friend
She tells the future
Like fantasies and fallacies.

I have a little friend
I love her and her heart
I have a little friend
She is a great gift.

Ghost

If my friend is a ghost
Then I am alone
And liable to be harmed.

If my child is a ghost
Then I am finished
And very dead.

If my father is a ghost
Then I am wayward
And backward.

If my mother is a ghost
Then I am lonely
And without love.

If my brother is a ghost
Then I am vulnerable
And devourable.

If my sister a ghost
Then I am lacking
And wanting and needing.

Cold

Come my lover
Come, bring me a cover
For I am cold.

Come, my lover
Come bring me love,
For I need the move.

Come, my friend
Come give me some gist
For I am folding my fist.

Come, my friend
Come speak to me,
For me, you need to see.

Come, my lover
Come with your staff
For my love is stiff.

Come, my lover
Come, I am cold
Come, warm me up.

God's Love

When I look at you
And look at me
I thank God for life
And for health.

When I look at you
And look at me,
I thank God for love
And for breath.

When I look at you
And look at me
I thank God for reality
And for unity.

When I look at you
And look at me
I thank God for vision
And for mission.

When I look at God
And His blessings
I thank Him for sovereignty
And supremacy.

Culture

Some people flog women
To prove their strength,
Some flog men
To know their energy
But I wonder and wonder
The crack in the lack.

Some cultures scare
Some cultures kill,
Some cultures dehumanize
Some terminate,
Some cultures are not cultures.

The people's way of life
Must not be by knife
The people's way of life
Must not be in strife.

Dear culture
If you are here to burn
Burn then in hell.

Religion

Crises abound
Wherever we go,
Troubles spread
Everywhere we live
But issues swell
Because of religion.

When religion is evil
Pushing for the devil,
Then it is ungodly
And can offer nothing holy.

Religion is a pit
Whoever wants to sit
Should receive a bit
So when we wail
Because we are frail
We lose the rail
And totally derail
Therefore our peace
Leaves us in some piece.

Chains

Chains are chains
Chains are rains,
Chains are pains
Chains are not gains.

Chains are strains
Chains are stains
Chains may not be bargains.

Chains are disdains
Chains are trains.

Chains are chains
Chains are mountains
Chains may not be fountains.

Chains are pains
Chains are chains
Chains chain chains.

Freeborn

I am a freeborn
Born free, born boundless
I am a freeborn
Born free, born unlimited.

If you see me in Asia
Call me a freeborn
If you see me in America,
If you see me in Europe
If you see me in Australia
Call me freeborn.

I am Africa
I am not a slave
I am chocolate
I am dark
I am fair
I am beautiful
I am brown
I am honey, I am rich
I flow with blessings
And spread richness
I am not bondage
I am a freeborn.

Angel

Dear angel
Spread your wings
Over my roof
Over my shelter,
Over my head.

Dear angel
Sprinkle your love
Over my life
Over my being
Over my future.

Dear angel
Guide my say
Guide my day,
Secure my bay
Guard my way
Protect where I lay
Be my ray.

Dear angel
I love you dearly
Please help me be an angel
So that we can bond best.

Happy Birthday

Happy birthday
Today and beyond
You were born, born to heal
O heal, seal, and be real.

Happy birthday
Today and beyond
May you live long
And bear fruits
Good fruits, blossoming and booming
Teeming and dominating.

Happy birthday
Welcome to the world
May you have peace and joy
May greatness locate you
May you reign like a king.

Happy birthday
Hurray, a god is born.

Rebirth

I pray for you today
May you have a rebirth,
A newness of life.

I pray for you now
May you be renewed
Beyond the oldness of life.

I pray for you today
May you regenerate
And sprout in the midst of rocks.

I pray for you always
May nothing hold you back
May the heavens favour you
May the spirits protect you
May everything refresh you
May life honour you
May all respect you.

I pray for you forever
I rebuke delay and death
Let there be a great rebirth.

Congratulations

Congratulations
You stand out
In the crowd, you shine
In the dark, you glitter
In the tunnel, you dazzle.

Congratulations
You are unique
In the spirit, you boom
In the flesh, you grow
In many realms, you blossom.

Congratulations
You are great
You have not come to scatter
Rather to gather,
You have not come to shatter
Rather to cater,
You have not come to batter
Rather to water
Congratulations
You are not here to flatter
You matter, not a hater
Not later, but for a glorious latter.

Parenting

A huge task
With burden so heavy,
A great job
With dreams so scary
Parenting, a dance of the gods.

Energy and vitality
Strength and disability
Hope and integrity
Vision and sincerity
Mission and capability
Parenting, a way of the brave.

The yearn for forwardness
The yarn for posterity
The yawn for maturity
Parenting, a cup of vigilance.

A mile so extra
A call for solemnity
A ladder for the gallant
A dive for safety
Parenting, a world of chances.

Emancipation

Here, it is
Our emancipation
Here, it is
Our freedom
Here, it is
Our world.

Never say no
Never doubt it,
Never belittle yourself
For this light shines
And this candle burns.

It is real
Here, to heal
It is true
Here, to glue
It is fresh
Upon our flesh,
So be it now
And forever.

Time

The time is now
To be free from cruelty
The time is now
To free humanity.

The time has come
To liberate our future
The time has come
To be liberated for the future.

Time is precious
Let no one waste it,
Time is golden
Let no one abuse it.

Time is great
It proves everything
Time is neat
It washes everything.

The time is now
Our time has come
Let us build this time.

Choice

It has a rhythm
Flowing round us,
It has a music
We must dance.

Choice, it has a voice
Telling us the point
It has a noise
Showing us the result.

Choice, it is a blueprint
Of our decision,
In hurry or in care
It is the map
Of our decision
In anger or in love.

Choice, it is a stage
And a dance floor
It is a hall of fame
Or a prison of shame.

Money

Money, the great old friend
That exalts the common man,
Money, the biased wave
That saves the dirty man.

Money, the caller, the answerer
The giver, the taker
The announcer, the redeemer
The Quaker, the baker
Money, the toy god.

Money, the comforter
The reformer and refiner
Money, the doer and the deed
The chaser and the purchaser
Money, the golden image.

The talking machine
And the healing magnet
The saving caterpillar
And the building giant.

Money, the skyscraper
The castle, the palace and the paradise.

Take Me to the Mountains

I know you love me
And care for me too,
I know you want me
And need me too.

I know I am yours
And you are mine,
I know I love you
And I really do.

But take me to the mountains
Let me see the valleys
So that I can watch the world
From the top.

Take me to the mountains
Where there are fountains
Take me there
Let me leave here,
For this place is hot
And I don't want to rot.

The mountains are peaceful
The mountains are joyful
They are godly
Let's go for transformation.

Marriage

I was taught about marriage
When I was tender
My teacher did,
It was a union, yes a union
Between a man and a woman.

 My teacher told me another
Of polygamy and polyandry
A man with more than one wife
And a woman with more than one husband.

Now, my teacher has gone
And someone has come
He taught me another
Marriage is a union
No, this time a different union
Between a man and a man
Between woman and woman
Between human and animal.

O my dear teacher
I wish you were here,
I miss you so dearly
For marriage reminds me of you.

Honey

You are my honey
I cannot buy with money,
You are my honey
I cannot drop for sugar.

Yes my honey
Believe me, it is true
You are my honey
That the bees cannot produce.

You are my honey
Honey from above,
You are my manna
Manna from heaven.

Honey, my dear
Manna, my bread
You feed me love
You feed me joy
You make me glow,
Glow, with pride
The sweetness of my life.

I humbly appreciate and acknowledge Onye Amarachi Valentine, the owner of AMARA'S FASHION HOUSE, located at No. 12 Apaogodo Street, off Ada George Road, Port Harcourt, Rivers State, Nigeria.

My sincere thanks to the staff:
Chinenye Ilochi
Blessing Eze
Blessing Obialo
Derima Enim
Hannah West
Chioma Okoronkwo
Blessing Olugbenle
Glory Oluo
Chioma Nkaa
Amara Nnosiri
Constance Ovodo

These people in less than one month of knowing and joining them have taught and are teaching me tailoring. Their comeliness and friendship is mind blowing.

about the author

Ngozi Olivia Osuoha is a Nigerian poet, writer and thinker. A graduate of Estate Management with experience in Banking and Broadcasting.

She has published nine poetry books and co-authored one (with Kenyan literary critic Amos O. Ojwang').

She has featured in more than forty international anthologies and also has published over two hundred and fifty poems and articles in over twenty countries.

Many of her poems have been translated and published into other languages, including Spanish, Romanian, Khloe, Farsi, and Arabic, among others.

She has won many awards; she is a one time *Best of the Net* nominee, and she has numerous words on marble.

www.ingramcontent.com/pod-product-compliance
Lightning Source LLC
Chambersburg PA
CBHW030103100526
44591CB00008B/257